CONTENTS

Introduction

I like cats. I used to have a lovely Silver and White **Tabby** cat called Barnaby. He was a **stray** and I had rescued him. Barnaby had one of his front teeth missing and he walked with a funny sort of wobble. He was special and I loved him.

One day he just disappeared and I never saw him again. I still miss him and I keep hoping that one day a silver and white Tabby with a tooth missing and a funny limp will be brought into my surgery and Barnaby will have come home.

People with cats care for and fuss over them a great deal, which is surprising really when you think that 'the cat' is still a bit of a wild animal.

Your cat will share your home but it will never let you forget just how independent it is.

MY PET

CAT

Nigel Taylor T.V. Vet

 LEARNING SUPPORT SERVICES

Please return on or before the last date stamped below

 City College NORWICH

MY PET

Titles in this series

Cat	Hamster
Dog	Mini Pets
Fish	Pony and Horse
Guinea Pig	Rabbit

To Michael and Cathryn

Title page Many people are cat lovers. It is not difficult to see why when they are so lovable.

Words in **bold** appear in the glossary.

Series editor: Geraldine Purcell
Designer: Jean Wheeler

© Copyright 1992 Wayland (Publishers) Ltd

First published in 1992 by Wayland (Publishers) Ltd,
61 Western Road, Hove, East Sussex, BN3 1JD, England

British Library Cataloguing in Publication Data
Taylor, Nigel
Cat. – (My Pet Series)
I. Title II. Gordon, Mike
III. Yates, John IV. Series
636.8

HARDBACK ISBN 0-7502-0329-3

PAPERBACK ISBN 0-7502-0925-9

Typeset by Dorchester Typesetting Group Ltd, Dorchester
Printed by G. Canale & C.S.p.A., Turin

Above Healthy, happy kittens like nothing better than playing with toys – even a piece of string will do!

Healthy kittens or cats

Check the following to see if your kitten or cat is healthy.

Eyes	Bright and clear with no discharge.
Ears	Clean with no discharge or sore areas.
Fur	Soft and silky. Dry and flaky fur is a sign of fleas.
Behaviour	Lively and interested in everything around them.

Right Cats are mysterious creatures. Their pretty faces, graceful movements and independent natures make them fascinating pets.

Cats in history

Above The cats of Ancient Egypt may have looked very like this regal Abyssinian cat.

The Ancient Egyptians were great cat lovers. About 4,000 years ago they were the first people to **domesticate** the cat. Modern Abyssinian cats probably look like the cats the Egyptians kept.

Cats were important to the Egyptians because they kept mice and rats out of their valuable grain stores. This task was so important that the Egyptian religion worshipped cats – when a cat died the whole family would go into mourning. The Egyptians even **mummified** their dead cats so that they too could share the life after death the Egyptians looked forward to. Today, you can see these cat mummies in museums all over the world.

Above Cats are great, natural hunters – which is bad news for mice, I'm sad to say.

The European cat was domesticated later, during Roman times. Again, the cat was important for protecting food stores.

Unfortunately, during the Middle Ages people feared sorcery and witchcraft and believed that cats were evil. Many cats were killed because of this. Cats became popular again during the Middle Ages when rats and mice carrying diseases plagued Europe and the only way to stop them was to **breed** cats to kill these pests.

Over the centuries, cats have been given a place in folklore and superstition – we have all heard that cats have nine lives and that if a black cat crosses your path it will bring good luck. I have tripped over a few in my time so I'm not so sure of that! It is the cat's mysterious nature that attracts many people to them, including me.

Choosing your cat

Opposite Cats, such as this Tabby, love to bask in the sunshine – especially if they can manage a few minutes catnap at the same time!

Cats are so independent and can have kittens so easily that there are a lot of **crossbreed** cats around. These, like my friend Barnaby, are called mongrels (or moggies) and are probably the most popular household cat.

Over the years, certain cats have been specially bred to keep certain features and markings pure. These cats are called **pedigrees**. There are over 100 varieties of pedigree cats, so you are spoilt for choice if you want one.

Remember, before you buy a cat, although they are independent and like to roam, cats do not like to be left alone or ignored all day while everybody is at school or work. Also, cats like to be able to come and go from the house whenever they want to – so a **cat flap** (see page 17) is essential. If your cat cannot come and go as it pleases, it may well try to find another household in which it can!

Cats and cars do not mix, so if you live near a very busy road then perhaps a cat is not the pet for you.

My pet cat

Cat **breeds** are divided into three main types: the Foreign short-haired (also called Orientals), the British (or European) short-haired and the British long-haired.

Foreign cats have long legs and lean bodies. They also have wedge-shaped heads, pointed ears and long, pointed tails. Perhaps you would like a cat that looks like those the Egyptians kept, the Abyssinian, which is a beautiful short-haired cat.

Another well-known Foreign short-haired cat is the elegant Siamese. Most Siamese have a pale, cream-coloured coat with their 'points' – ears, legs, face and tail – in various darker shades.

The Burmese cat and the Havana (a lovely, chocolate-brown coloured cat) are also popular. If you want a cat that looks a bit like E.T. when it is a kitten, then go for the Rex breeds. Rexes have closely-cropped, crinkly fur – the Devon and Cornish Rexes are good examples.

Above The Siamese is one of the most popular Foreign cats in the world.

Below This pair of Rex kittens are a bit odd-looking – but very cute!

Above The British Blue cat is one of my favourites because it looks so cuddly!

The most famous British short-haired cat is the Manx cat. These lovely, strongly-built cats are born without a tail. One of my favourite short-haired varieties is the British Blue. These are so pretty they look like cuddly toys!

British cats have broad heads with very rounded features. They have shorter legs and thicker bodies than the Foreign breeds. This type of stocky body shape is often called 'cobby'.

Above Long-haired cats, like this Ginger Persian, need daily grooming (see page 21). Making time to do this task every day may seem a bit of a chore but when you see how smart your cat looks afterwards – it will be well worth the effort.

If you have plenty of time, patience and have ambitions to be a hairdresser later on, then why not try a long-haired cat? These are often called Persians. They have a cobby body but have a fluffy coat with a full, bushy tail. Persians can come in many colours but the cream and the blue are the best known.

These days, there are also foreign long-haired cats, such as the Balinese (a long-haired Siamese) and the Somali (a long-haired Abyssinian).

So there you are – lots of choice. A word of warning though – White cats with blue eyes are deaf, but other than that are perfectly healthy and make lovely pets.

Above This Blue-point Siamese is a fine example of a Foreign cat.

Above A mischievous Tortoiseshell and White British short-haired cat.

Above This is a very grand looking Black Persian cat.

Main cat breeds

Type:	Description:	Examples:
Foreign (Oriental) Short-haired	Lean bodies. Wedge-shaped heads. Pointed ears and tails.	Abyssinian Burmese Egyptian Mau Foreign Lilac Foreign White Havana Rex Russian Blue Siamese
British (European) Short-haired	Thick-set. Short legs. Broad head, rounded features.	Bicoloured Black Blue Cream British Blue Cream Manx Spotled Tabby Tortoiseshell Tortoiseshell and White White (with blue or orange eyes)
British (European) Long haired	Thick-sel. Short legs. Fluffy coat. Full tail.	Bicoloured Black Blue Blue Cream Brown Cameo Chinchilla Cream Lilac Red Smoke Tabby Tortoiseshell Tortoiseshell and White White (with blue or orange eyes)

A home for your cat

Above Cats are very clever animals – but they can be very naughty as well! Cats are always curious, so you have to make sure that they don't search out adventure behind the TV set or near other electrical equipment in your home.

Your vet should be able to tell you where to find the local pedigree cat breeders. He or she will also be able to tell you where to find the nearest animal rescue centres, run by organizations such as the **R.S.P.C.A.** Sometimes, advertisements in the newspapers will lead you to a healthy **litter**.

You should decide before going to see a litter if you want a male or a female kitten, and if you might want to breed from your cat.

Most vets and animal welfare groups would discourage breeding crossbreed cats because there are so many already and there are a great number of strays. To stop this problem it is advised to have pet cats **neutered**. This will also stop some trouble and irritation for you later on (see box below).

If you want to check the sex of a kitten then you have to look under its tail. Female kittens have two holes, close together. Male kittens have two holes further apart.

Neutering

- Neutering your cat will mean it cannot ever have kittens.

- It is a simple operation and will not harm your pet at all.

- Female kittens should be **spayed** at sixteen weeks old.

- Male kittens should be neutered at thirty-six weeks old.

Will neutering change my cat's behaviour?
The answer is yes – but for the better. An unneutered male (tom) cat marks his **territory** – that is your house – by spraying **urine**. Not very pleasant! This will not happen once he is neutered. An unspayed female (queen) makes loud '**calling**' noises when she is in season (ready to mate and have kittens). This too will stop once she is spayed.

When you go to see a litter of kittens, try to see them with the mother. It is best not to take a kitten away from the mother until it is fully **weaned** at around eight weeks old. Pick the liveliest kitten of the colour you prefer.

You should check your kitten for the basic healthy signs (see page 5) but also take it to your vet for a thorough examination.

Your kitten will need its first **vaccinations** against the major cat diseases (see page 27) when it is nine weeks old and its second injection at twelve weeks old. If you get a kitten between these ages then the litter's owners should be able to provide you with a vaccination certificate. You can keep this up-to-date with the annual **booster injections**.

Above It is very easy to fall in love with a cute little kitten – they are all so lovely. But, take your time when you are choosing your pet and make sure that you have made arrangements for the new arrival before you take your kitten home.

A new kitten in a new home

There are some things you can do to prepare for your kitten coming to live with you.

Bedding

Kittens like to feel secure and warm. Your kitten will need a comfortable place to catnap to make it feel at home. You can buy a cat basket or plastic bed and put a cushion inside to make it cosy. Make sure that the cushion is washable. Place the kitten's bed in a warm place out of a draught and somewhere where trampling human feet will not intrude.

Below Cats are naturally very clean animals. They soon learn to use their litter trays.

Litter trays

You will also need a litter tray. Cats are very clean animals and like to dig a hole for their mess and then cover it up. You can start training your kitten to do this when it is three weeks old. It is a good idea to put some earth into the tray as well as the shop-bought litter-grit or sand, because the kitten will then link the idea of doing its mess in the earth out in the garden when it is older.

Toys

Cats and kittens love toys. Playing with them helps your kitten to learn hunting skills and will keep it lively and active. Buy proper pet shop toys because they have been tested for safety.

Right Cat flaps are great for those cats who love a night on the tiles!

Above Cats love to play with their pet toys, such as plastic balls and cloth mice.

Cat flaps

When your kitten is a bit older and has had all of the vaccinations, it will want to explore the outside world. It is in a cat's nature to roam but it will normally keep fairly close to its home – if only to pop in for its meal and a catnap before a night on the tiles! So, a cat flap on an outside door is very important.

Leave it to an adult who knows a lot about woodwork to put in the cat flap as they are very tricky. The only trouble with a cat flap is that strange cats might visit. I have found that the best flaps to stop this are those with magnetic strips which keep the flap shut until your cat, with its own magnetic collar, comes and pushes it open.

My pet cat

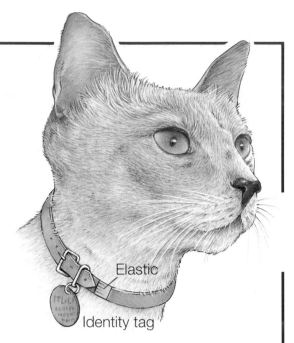

Collars

You should get your kitten used to a collar as soon as possible. The best ones are the elasticated ones which will not choke your kitten or cat if it gets caught up on something while your pet is out exploring. Remember to put a tag with your name and address on the collar so if your cat gets lost it can be returned to you.

Elastic

Identity tag

Above Elasticated collars are the safest type for your cat.

Scratching posts

Your kitten or cat will need to sharpen its claws on something. Give your pet its own scratching post so that it does not choose the brand new sofa to rip to bits. Scratching posts are usually made of wood and are covered with some hardwearing material, such as sack cloth or a piece of carpet.

Below You can make your own scratching post for your cat.

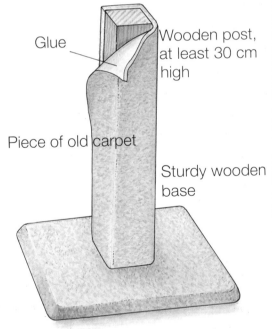

Glue

Wooden post, at least 30 cm high

Piece of old carpet

Sturdy wooden base

Left Cats sharpen their claws a lot. This one is using a dead branch – that's better than your new sofa!

Training and handling your cat

Training

Training your kitten to use a litter tray should be fairly straightforward. If it does have the occasional accident in the wrong place do not follow the old wives' tale of rubbing your kitten's nose in the mess to show it was wrong. In fact your kitten will think the opposite and will use that place all the time – even if it is your slippers! Instead clean up the mess thoroughly and put your kitten on the litter tray.

Cats are very independent creatures. They need their freedom, so cat flaps are a good idea. The trouble is that not all kittens and cats take to them straight away. For the first few times you may have to help and encourage your pet to go through. Your cat will soon learn to jump through the cat flap quickly just in case it catches its tail. Very undignified! Once it has the hang of it there will be no stopping your cat!

Handling

When a cat wants your company you will soon know it. Your cat will rub itself against your legs or jump on to your lap. You will soon learn to judge your cat's moods – when a cat wants to be friendly it is very friendly and when it wants to be left alone you should do exactly that. Do not try to cuddle your sleeping cat or spend hours coaxing it from the top of the wardrobe.

Right There's nothing cats like better than a cuddle. Be careful always to handle your cat gently and to support its weight by putting your hand or arm around its back legs.

Below Instead of carrying your cat to the car or to the vet in your arms, it is much safer to take your cat in a proper cat carrier or a box with air-holes in it.

Most cats do like to be held or stroked. You will have to get your kitten used to being picked up and handled, the earlier you start the more sociable your grown cat will be. But you must make sure that you always handle your kitten or cat properly, so that it feels secure in your arms. I see so many people picking up their cats with their hands around the cat's shoulder area only, and leaving the rear (hind) legs dangling. This is the wrong way to pick up a cat.

When lifting a cat you should put one hand underneath the chest and the other hand around the rear legs. This way you will be able to support the cat's weight and it will feel much safer.

Sometimes you will have to take your cat on journeys by car or bus or walking. You should always put your cat into a cat carrier or a cardboard box with a lid and air holes when taking it from the house to the vet or **cattery**, for example. Never let your cat travel loose in a car because it will be frightened and may distract the driver.

Grooming

Cats are very clean and tidy creatures and really enjoy preening themselves with their paws and licking their fur.

Short-haired cats do not really need to be groomed. Long-haired cats need a lot of help with this job. You will have to set aside time every day to groom your Persian cat – at least fifteen minutes. Use a soft brush or a wide-toothed comb and always brush in the direction of the fur.

Cats usually **moult** twice a year. At these times even short-haired cats will need a little help with grooming. Grooming your cat during its moulting period will stop all the furniture and your clothes being covered in little hairs. It also lessens the chances of your cat getting very bad **fur-balls** in its stomach.

While you are grooming your cat you can check its health. To know what to look out for, see the box on page 5 and the 'Keeping your cat healthy' section on pages 27–29.

Grooming kit

You will need:
A soft brush
A wide-toothed comb
Flea powder

Always be very gentle with your cat while you are grooming it and talk to your cat so that it feels loved and pampered.

Left This cat is enjoying being groomed. Moulting fur must make your cat feel very itchy so sometimes even short-haired cats need a little help.

Feeding your cat

Chews

Tinned
cat food

Dry
food

Soft
moist
food

Above There are a lot of different types of cat food that you can buy. Your cat will soon make it clear which type it prefers.

Right Some bossy kittens just don't like sharing their tasty dinners. It is not very fair is it!

Feeding cats is quite easy. Today there are many tinned and dried foods on sale for kittens and cats, which are ideal. Always make sure that there is water available for a kitten or cat being fed on dry foods. Cats do not normally lap up lots of water but they should have a dish of water there if they want it.

Feeding kittens

Once your kitten is weaned from its mother's milk it will need three or four small meals a day. Kittens have small stomachs so they need to be fed little and often. A young kitten will be used to drinking its mother's milk so it will need a dish of milk with its meal. I find that cow's milk does sometimes give kittens and cats upset stomachs. If you are worried about this then ask your vet for advice about using babies' powdered milk instead. By the time your cat is six months old it does not really need milk anyway.

Left Lots of cats do love to lap up a saucer of milk – but they don't really need it if they are well-fed and healthy.

Feeding cats

Adult cats are usually easy to please. Cats are meat-eaters and enjoy chicken and lamb. Of course cats love fish too.

If you are giving your cat fresh meat then it should be cooked. Make sure there are no bones in the meat or fish. You should also chop up the meat very finely before serving it to your cat.

If the idea of cooking all your cat's meals is a problem, do not worry. I find that most cats are perfectly happy and healthy when they are fed on tinned or dried foods. Maybe your cat would like the occasional treat of fresh meat once or twice a week. Do not feed your cat offal, such as heart, liver or kidney, as too much leads to problems with the bones.

Your kitten or cat will be able to 'tell' you how much food it wants at each meal – by simply leaving some and walking away or pestering you for more. Do not leave old food in your cat's bowl as it will not go near stale food. Always wash out the bowl and if your cat did leave some food then give it a little less for the next meal until you find the amount your cat is happy with.

Breeding your cat

Female cats that have not been spayed are called queens. Queens are in season several times a year. Female cats that are ready to mate make lots of loud noises to call male (tom) cats to them. Female cats can come into season by the time they are six months old, so unspayed females should be separated from unneutered males from this age.

Many cat **pregnancies** are unplanned, so it may be difficult for you to know if your cat is pregnant or not – this is the chance you take with letting an unspayed female cat outside, I'm afraid. Good signs to look for are the reddening of her **nipples** and noticing if she is getting a bit fatter. Do not start prodding your cat's stomach to see. If she is pregnant you may cause some damage and even if she is not she may not take kindly to being poked!

If your female cat does mate with a male the pregnancy will last about nine weeks. The mother-to-be should be given extra food and water during the pregnancy. She will also need extra vitamins and minerals to keep in good health. Your vet will be able to advise you on what to give her.

Below right You can make your own kittening box out of an old cardboard box, or wood if you are good at woodwork.

Cut out front section

Cushion

Newspaper

Queens give birth quite easily. They choose warm, comfortable places in the house to have their kittens. You could make a kittening box out of any cardboard box in which your cat can move around and lie down comfortably. Cut away the front section of the box so that your cat can walk into it easily – when she is heavily pregnant she will not want to leap very much! Line the bottom of the box with newspaper and put a washable, soft cushion or rug inside to make the bed cosy.

Left Cats make great mums. This proud mother is happily suckling (feeding) her seven new-born kittens.

Your cat will choose the place she wants to have her kittens so put the box there. Do not worry if she changes her mind a few times or decides that she does not want the kittening box at all. You should leave your cat alone while she is giving birth but if you are worried or if this is your cat's first litter then your vet should be able to give you advice and help if necessary. The kittens should be ready to suckle milk from their mother immediately. Once you have checked that mother and kittens are fine then leave the new family alone to get used to each other.

Your cat will be a bit tired after the birth but should perk up in a few hours and like to eat.

Left Kittens soon grow up. These seven-week-old kittens look a real handful don't they? They are nearly ready to leave their mother and go to new homes.

Kittens are born with closed eyes and their ears folded back so they cannot see or hear. They rely totally on their mother for food, warmth and safety. By the time they are five to ten days old their eyes are partly open. At three weeks old their eyes are completely open and they are walking and beginning to play and explore. Your kittens will begin to eat solid food at about three weeks old and are totally weaned by eight weeks.

You will have to find homes for the kittens when they are weaned. You could ask family or friends or your could put advertisements in local newspapers or your vet's surgery.

Finding good homes for all the kittens may be very hard and this is why animal welfare groups like the R.S.P.C.A. and most vets would advise owners to have their cats neutered (see page 14).

Breeding

● A female cat can have up to nine kittens in a litter – would you be able to find good homes for all of them?

● If you have a pedigree cat then you will want to mate him or her with another cat of the same breed – your vet may know of someone locally or can put you in touch with a cat club that specializes in your cat's breed.

● A queen cat can have many litters and is ready to go into season soon after giving birth to her previous litter.

● Constant pregnancies will begin to affect your cat's health and are not advised.

Keeping your cat healthy

Vaccinations

Kittens get a lot of protection against diseases from their mother's milk. This helps them in the early weeks of life. This natural protection does not last very long and that is why your kitten will need vaccinations. At nine weeks old, kittens need to have their first vaccination against the major cat illnesses – feline enteritis and cat flu. The second vaccination is given at twelve weeks.

Feline enteritis

This unpleasant illness attacks the cat's bowel. Once a cat gets feline enteritis it will die within a few hours – even if a vet is called.

Cat flu

This illness can kill as well. Cat flu causes a lot of discomfort and distress to the suffering kitten or cat. The first signs of cat flu are that the cat will sneeze and sniff and go off its food. Really bad cases develop pneumonia (a chest infection). The cat may also get sores and blisters inside its nose and on its tongue.

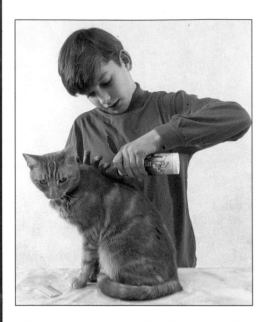

Above Cats don't like flea powder very much but they have to learn to put up with it if they want to be flea-free! Take care *not* to puff the powder into your cat's eyes.

Fleas
Fleas are a big problem for cats and their owners. Flea sprays and powders are very good at getting rid of them. The trouble is that cats do not like being squirted with the stuff very much! If you have a long-haired cat, then you will be able to apply the spray or powder while you are grooming it. If you do not groom your cat very much then put your pet on a table and hold your cat firmly but gently by the **scruff** of the neck. Spray the fur but make sure that you avoid your cat's eyes.

You will also need to spray the flea powder on to your cat's bed and any place in the house it likes to rest.

Ticks
Ticks are parasites and they can be a real nuisance. They are greyish-white and burrow into the cat's skin. To remove a tick spray the area with flea powder to kill it first then pull it out using a pair of tweezers. You have to make sure that the head of the tick comes out of the cat's skin or it will cause a sore patch.

Ringworm
Ringworm (a fungal **parasite**) is common on cats. An infected cat will have patchy fur loss and *even* a few scabs on the skin. Your vet will give you some ointment to clear up the infection. You must always wash your hands after handling a cat with ringworm as it can be passed on to humans.

Eyes
Cats often get red, sore eyes – especially when they have been fighting and have been scratched on the face. Your vet will give you some eye drops to clear up *eye* infections.

Ears

From time to time you should check your cat's ears to make sure they are clean and do not have anything in them, such as grass seeds, which may lead to an ear infection. If you do find something in there, do not poke around inside your cat's ears yourself – let your vet do that.

Worms

All kittens and cats should be regularly wormed against roundworm (a parasite). Cats often get tapeworms (another parasite) as well. Tapeworms grow inside the cat's body and use up most of the goodness in the food the cat has eaten. This means that the cat will become very weak if the tapeworms are not removed. You can get worming tablets from a pet shop or a vet.

Upset stomachs

Cats often get upset stomachs. Usually it is because they have eaten something they cannot digest. If your cat has an upset stomach then do not feed it for one day. For the next five days feed your cat boiled fish, chicken and rice. Do not give it milk. If the condition does not get better then go to your vet.

Your vet

Most vets love working with cats. All kittens and cats should be vaccinated and have booster injections every year.

Enjoy your cat.

Glossary

Booster injections The yearly injections which vaccinate cats against diseases they can pick up from other cats and animals, such as cat flu. The vaccination does not last forever so your cat will need a boost or top-up of the protection.

Breed To mate a male (tom) and female (queen) cat to produce kittens.

Breeds The many different types of cat. Each breed can be recognized because of a very strong feature, such as the long hair of the Persian cats.

Calling An unspayed female cat, also called a queen, will make loud noises and act in a very strange way during her season – when she is prepared to mate. This odd behaviour is called 'calling'.

Cat flap A specially designed door which is fixed into an outside door of a house. It allows a cat to come and go from the house.

Cattery A place which will keep your cat for a short time, for example when you are away on holiday and cannot take your cat too. All good catteries will need proof that your cat has been vaccinated before they will let your pet stay.

Crossbreed The type of kitten which comes from the mating of two different breeds of cat. A kitten which has more than two breeds in its family line is called a mongrel or moggy.

Domesticate To train a wild animal to trust and work with a human.

Fur-balls The balls of fur which a cat builds up in its stomach because it has licked and swallowed its fur while grooming itself.

Litter A group of young kittens.

Moult The natural loss of old fur so that it can be replaced with fresh, new fur. All furry animals moult once or twice a year.

Mummified The Ancient Egyptians mummified the bodies of the dead by wrapping them up in cloth before burying them.

Neutered Cats are neutered to stop them being able to have kittens. The operation is performed by a vet and is called castration for male cats and spaying for female cats.

Nipples Also called teats, these are two rows of slightly raised flesh which run along the belly of your female cat. Kittens drink their mother's milk from these teats.

Parasite An animal which lives on another animal's body.

Pedigrees The cats whose families' history has a long line of purebred cats of the same breed.

Pregnancies When female (queen) cats are carrying kittens inside their bodies.

R.S.P.C.A. The Royal Society for the Prevention of Cruelty to Animals. A leading British animal welfare organization.

Scruff The loose flesh on the back of a cat's neck.

Spayed When a female (queen) cat has been neutered so that she cannot have any kittens.

Stray A homeless cat which has become semi-wild.

Tabby A breed of cat which has very striking stripes along its fur.

Territory The area which cats mark out around their home which they guard and protect from other cats' use.

Urine The liquid waste which comes from animals' bodies. Male (tom) cats use their urine to mark out their territory.

Vaccinations The series of injections which put a weakened form of a disease into your kitten which will stop your pet from getting the full-blown disease.

Weaned When a kitten has stopped taking its mother's milk and is eating solid foods.

Further reading

For younger readers:
Care for your Cat, by Tina Hearne (Collins, 1985)
My First Kitten, by Nigel Taylor (Firefly Books, 1991)
The Going Live! Cat Book, by Grace McHattie (BBC Books, 1990)

For older readers:
Cats (Know Your Pet series) by Anna and Michael Sproule (Wayland, 1988)
The Going Live! Pet Book, by Nigel Taylor (BBC Books, 1989)
The Ultimate Cat Book, by David Taylor (Dorling Kindersley, 1989)

Useful addresses

American Society for the Prevention of Cruelty to Animals (A.S.P.C.A.), 441 E. 92nd St., New York, NY 10028, USA
Cat Association of Great Britain, Hunting Grove, Lowfield Heath, Crawley, West Sussex, RH11 0PY, England

The Royal Society for the Prevention of Cruelty to Animals (R.S.P.C.A.), The Manor House, Horsham, West Sussex, RH12 1HG, England
The Toronto Humane Society, 11 River St., Toronto, Ontario, M5A 4C2, Canada

Index

Picture acknowledgements

Bruce Coleman Ltd/ (J Burton) 10 (top), 13 (centre), 16, 18, 20 (bottom), 22, 25, 26/(J Fryer) 7/
(H Reinhard) 11, 12, 13 (bottom); Oxford Scientific Films Ltd/(G I Bernard) 14/(S Dalton) 23/
(R Packwood) 17/(R Pearcy/Animals Animals) 6/(H Reinhard/Okapia) 5/(B Schellhammer/Okapia) 9;
Tony Stone Worldwide/*cover*, 10 (bottom); WPL/(Z Mukhida) title page, 20 (top), 21, 28;
ZEFA 13 (top).